WHY THE SEA IS SALT

WHY THE SEA IS SALT
Poems of Love and Loss

Kirkpatrick Sale

Writers Club Press
San Jose New York Lincoln Shanghai

WHY THE SEA IS SALT
Poems of Love and Loss

Writers Club Press
an imprint of iUniverse.com, Inc.

For information address:
iUniverse.com, Inc.
5220 S 16th, Ste. 200
Lincoln, NE 68512
www.iuniverse.com

ISBN: 0-595-17640-2

Printed in the United States of America

WHY THE SEA IS SALT

Rain is but the tears of stars

That weep for some remembered fault,

And that is why the hills erode,

The hopes and loves of men corrode,

And why the sea is salt.

I

LOVE

*

Little did you know

When opening that gate

The flood there was behind.

Now you see the flow

And know how great.

Please be, drowning, kind.

DARK EYES

1.

I watched you, tender as a fawn,

Look up startled, dark eyes searching

Reassurance, as fawns do, urging

All in place before moving on.

There is no place, only places.

Chances elaborate within

Themselves, unbidden, dreams can begin

As sighs and end as distant faces.

For, love, there are no sanctuaries

In the constancy of conflicting wants,

And the silent dark without response

That waits us there forever varies.

And there, ahead, all we know

Is as insubstantial as a sigh

Before sleep: I would not try

To knit the clouds, or capture snow.

From too long lingering in tall shadows

I've learned the way of wants strangled

In place. But I watched you, and the languid

Wind was warm across those meadows.

2.

I watched you, dark eyes growing soft

With something deep and tentative

A man who needed such a gift

Might be forgiven for calling love,

Although I would not ever plead

That it be love: let it be

No more than what I think I see,

My need reflected in your need,

Which doesn't ask a name, any more

Than flowers do, or stars; let

It be what it becomes, not what

We thought we used to dream before.

But know that in them I have found

The sweet regenerative thing

That allowed at last a sensuous spring

To rush into a dormant land.

3.

In those dark eyes, which start to sparkle

With the newness of desire, I watch

The tide that fills my harbor, and catch

The rays of dawn against my darkness.

The voice of your eyes is sudden thunder

Deeper than valleys, and in the roar

Of their passion I wait listening for

The echo of my own wild wonder.

*

Yes, there's danger here that can't be disregarded,

But please believe there's nothing you need to feel a guilt for:

It's true that ships are safest when they're in the harbor,

But that is not what they were built for.

It is not wrong, however fearsome now and daunting,

To think that we can find a world where love suffices:

All explorations must be done with care and caution,

But some discover paradises.

WHY THE SEA IS SALT

*

Who needs a love affair

So acrid sweet and wild and tortuous

It takes us, heedless, God knows where

On one of those miraculous

Adventures that can change a life? Beware:

Apparently, both of us.

"WILL WE STILL BE FRIENDS?"

Just because the trail ascends beyond the highlands

Into the mountains lost in clouds, and still beyond

Where no one knows the land, or where the pathway ends,

Doesn't mean the lovers starting out, in awkward silence,

With first uncertain steps and slow, will not have found,

No matter where the journey's done, that they're still friends.

WHY THE SEA IS SALT

*

A bit naïve

To think you haven't dazzled others all this while:

Lips that always seem about to whisper "please,"

Eyes that sparkle with summer-morning-sunshine rays

Then darken with a sudden quiet knowing ease

As if you're seeing into a heart's most secret place.

Please believe

There's not a man whose knees don't buckle at your smile.

I ought to know,

For didn't I try in all those meetings to resist you,

As you opened more of you, and—wonder—more of me,

Knowing what would happen if in fact we crossed

That line between still-friends and lovers-that-might-be?

And now, even after all these days, I haven't lost

The vertigo

That started in my knees the inevitable day I kissed you.

You've gone inside that part within me, she said,

Where no on ever dared to go before.

In truth, it was a place not hard to find:

"I need, I love" emblazoned on the door.

I knocked with just a gentle kiss or two

And felt her melt into some welcome part

That only then I knew to be that lonely

Inner place marked "Me, too" on my heart.

WHY THE SEA IS SALT

*

She pointed out that raptors,

Despite their reputation,

Descend with truly magisterial

Design, their gracious way

Of spelling out the chapters

In Nature's statutes of predation

Before they give their stark material

Decision to the prey.

She did not add that women

Can be quite the equal of

Those birds within their own raptorial

Designs, and who would say

It's different though the human

Sentencing is done for love:

Comestible or amatorial,

Either way there's prey.

JAPONICA

Only seventeen

Syllables to celebrate

Her whole volumned soul.

The necessity

Of your deliquescent eyes

Glistening with mine.

Pouting lip, perfect

Smile, perpetuating kiss—

Why would one want words?

However lovely,

Slight and delicately wrought,

No poem matches you.

JAPONICA II

A soft, insouciant

Cloud declares itself across

One insistent star.

Butterflies—of course—

Signal with their slowing wings

The waning summer.

Late at night I see

Your eyes go wide with wonder

When at last I come.

*

What have an old man's rescuings

Of youth to do with love? Hasn't he

Some self-respect, and dignity

Enough to keep his febrile doings

To himself—or at least away

From unprotected hearts? His hoary

Fingers seek compensatory

Life in some remembered play

Where he does not, not now, belong.

Nor does it, finally, make him young.

I used to wonder why you'd see

An aged, pointed buck cavort

With some proscribed doe, for sport,

During hunting season, recklessly

Exposed as if he didn't care

WHY THE SEA IS SALT

That life was far too short to have

Such heedless arabesques of love

And hunters might be anywhere,

A careless giving-in to hunger.

I wonder that, alas, no longer.

after D.

Times past, I went prowling

Beside the shrouded walk,

Haphazard, urgently,

By faint stars I'd stalk;

Alone by choosing to be,

I moved as ferrets move;

All night long I was howling

Selfish, scorning love.

You came along, intending

Nothing more than a quiet

Stroll beside the walk,

And heard my heart's riot;

You thought to tame, with talk,

WHY THE SEA IS SALT

With love, to pacify.

And see: it is your befriending

Makes my howl a sigh.

*

Yes, I should be the "frivolous" affair you say

You ought to have, as insubstantial as the winds,

As unremembered as a February day.

But I'm afraid I've gone beyond that point long since:

Too late to think of you the gone-tomorrow way.

Yours have become the kisses with which my life begins.

WHY THE SEA IS SALT

*

Do not wake the griffon we've created

With our ardent touches, these urgent lips;

Let its full-maned passion, still unsated,

Hold us fixed within its taloned grips.

Do not wake it, to see if it is well:

Enough that, as it lies there, so it seems.

Please believe in what the ancients tell:

It is asleep, and we are the dream it dreams.

*

Lust you call it, lust indeed it is—

"Middle English **luste**, from the German

Lust, meaning pleasure, more at bliss"—

Bliss beyond what I had thought was human

To have, in the perfect body of a woman

Awakening me to lust—"akin to **lyste**,

Icelandic for desire"—the desire is

To consume myself inside you, to illumine

You with me, to commemorate the moment

Of your tumultuous lust—"akin to **list**,

Archaic English, to please"—to ease the famine

Of a heart too long without a love like this.

A lust past lust, a strange amalgam of

This bliss, desire, pleasure—and, yes, love.

WHY THE SEA IS SALT

*

In wildness is salvation, Thoreau said.

I don't think, though, he meant this hurricane

That whirls incessantly inside my head

And fills my heart with this torrential

frenzied, hungry, mad,

expectant, riotous, erotic,

painful

rain.

Oh, loved one, when will you be in my bed

And I can feel you in my arms again?

*

You can dismiss all this as only

Self-indulgence, which it is,

Practiced by a man whose lonely

Moments make his happiness,

Or as a kind of false remembrance,

Which it also is, a piece

Of posturing to make a man's

Administrations match his needs,

Or conjurations of desire

From one who's living in a past

Whose promises and passions were

Not half what he recalls them as.

Yes, yes, it is all of that,

And hardly what I'm proudest of.

But it is something more than that:

It is also, it is also love.

*

It is not making love, for that is made

Already, and grows, as dreams and rivers grow,

By itself; it is instead a way to show

This overwhelming wholeness, to celebrate

The depths of joy no words are capable of.

How yawpish paleolithic are the few

Bare sounds I have to intimate to you

The Shakespearian totality of my love;

The skin, the flesh, the pores, the very genes

Must demonstrate the depth of love by more

Than rhetoric—as politics and war,

A "carrying out of the same by other means."

The wonder is our bodies learn to transmit

The words of love when there are no words for it.

*

Time and circumstance distends us,

Now these miles apart,

And days we shared grow dimmer now,

Receding to the heart—

But has the press of my lips upon

Your sweet cunt clung

As strong as the salty taste of you

Still lingers on my tongue?

WHY THE SEA IS SALT

*

I felt you think of me last night.

I knew, though you are so far away:

I felt your kisses over me

As if some wild summer sea

Suffused me with its salty spray.

There are so many ways to show

The senses of a heart's delight,

But I'm content you came to me

As salty spray from a wild sea

Rises through a moonlit night.

*

When I awoke just now, the moon that sent

Me to bed at one, glaring untiring bright,

Was fading in the trees, anemic, spent,

Exhausted by her circuit of the night.

I'd given her a weary time of it, no doubt:

I'd made her prove her talent genuine

By beaming thoughts of you for hours out

And bringing distant thoughts from you back in.

And that could be the kind of task that any

Orb, though well-disposed, might tire of—

All the passion back and forth, and many

Anguished groans, and kisses, and sighs of love.

But still: I'm now awake. I don't see why

She has to go so soon while I'm still here,

And needy. Still there the whole expanse of sky

For her to range—why must she disappear?

WHY THE SEA IS SALT

*

I do not need to feel the stinging nettle

Of the rose to bleed and fall into its spell:

For that the softest brush of any petal

Does as well.

It does not take the biting winter torrent

Of the wind to turn my hands, or heart, to ice:

For that the mildest April undercurrent

Will suffice.

I do not need the fullest phosphorescence

Of the moon to ache with unforgotten love:

For that the thumbnail of its pale decrescence

Is enough.

I live stripped naked, bare to the sensations

Of the world, unarmored by the guise of art,

That I may better feel the least vibrations

Of your heart.

*

"Precious gems are diamonds, sapphires,
emeralds, and rubies. All others are
semi-precious. Precious jewels are
those which are brought to perfection
by the lapidary's art."—Retail Jewelers of America

Because it was, however lovely, all too brief,

An incandescent passion that before we knew

Became as full of promises as spring, and grew

Into that lovers' willful-suspension-of-disbelief;

Because you are so far away, and my relief

So long in coming, and all I have to see me through

Is memory, wine, a faded photograph of you,

And poems that celebrate my self-indulgent grief;

Is it any wonder that mostly what I do

At night is picture you a flawless counterpart

To all my dreams, a precious, perfect beauty who,

In spite of knowing better, loves me with all her heart?

Precious jewels are only those which must be brought

To their perfection by the lapidary's art.

WHY THE SEA IS SALT

*

Love, the French, who claim to know, declare

Is *une exchange de deux fantasies,*

And thus go on glowering gallicly about

Tristesse inevitable and *tragedies.*

All right, so be it: where better to live

Than Dream, for those who conjugate in Dream

And know that in its too-brief life, love

Is not sustained by *is* but *may* and *seem?*

What better barter than passion for escape,

Hope for hunger, ambition for desire?

Living out, and in, and with, illusion

Can do for love what wind can do for fire.

What better could the gods have done: and if

They hadn't planned to teach us self-deceit

Why would they make the moon so far away,

The turbulences of the heart so sweet?

So give me no *tristesse*, Pierre: *amour*

May have its dark delusions, right enough,

But didn't you know that they are indispensable

To make the bright invention that is love?

Shakespeare 147

My love is a fever still, longing still

For more of the same disease that sickened it,

Feeding on that source that makes it ill

And anguished, indulging in its fevered fit.

My reason, which tried to doctor to my love,

Has left me, angry that its recipe

Was disregarded, and desperate now I prove

Desire is death, and let that doctor me.

I am past cure, and with my reason gone

And frantic mad, I ache with love, and rave

As foolish madmen rave unseemly on,

With no more sense of truth than madmen have.

For I have sworn you fair, and thought you bright,

Who are really black as hell and dark as night.

PERSISTENCE

I wonder if it's wise to send so many

Letters, poems, notes, and cards to you,

Day after day, relentless, without any

Thought to what such constancy might do.

I read once of a lover in Mandalay,

Who, gripped by passion deeper far than most men,

Wrote his sweetheart every single day.

She ended up by marrying the postman.

VERLAINE—I

Votre ame est un paysage choisi

Que vont charmant manques et bergamasques,

Jouant du luth, et dansant, et quasi

Tristes sous leurs deguisements fantasques.

Tout en chantant sur le mode mineur

L'amour vainqueur et la vie opportune,

Ils n'ont pas l'air de croire a leur bonheur

Et leur chanson se mele au clair de lune,

Au calme clair de lune triste et beau,

Qui fait rever oiseaux les arbres

Et sangloter d'extase les jets d'eau

Les grands jets d'eau sveltes parmi les marbres.

1.

Your soul is like a chosen plot of land

Where dancers masked and bergamasks delight,

Playing upon their lutes, and dancing, and

A little sad in their fantastic rite.

They sing together, in a minor key,

Of love that conquers, life that's opportune;

They do not seem to believe their fortuity

And their song is mingled with the light of the moon,

With the calm light of the moon, sad and lonely,

That makes the birds in the trees go dreaming on,

And makes the fountains sob in ecstasy,

The great, sleek fountains amid the stones.

2.

Your soul is like a special place of earth

Where the dancers of my soul find their delight,

And play and frisk and gambol for all they're worth

To celebrate the glory of this night.

At times their song is sad , a minor key,

To think that morning's coming all too soon;

At times the notes are wild with gaiety

To know their song is mingled with the moon,

With the calm light of the moon, full and lovely,

That makes two souls unite across the miles

And distant hearts to sob in ecstasy,

Distant hearts, and souls, that join in smiles.

VERLAINE—II

Voici des fruits, des fleurs, des feuilles et des branches,

Et puis voici mon coeur, qui ne bat que pour vous.

Ne le dechirez pas avec vos deux mains blanches

Et qu'a vos yeux si beaux l'humble present soit doux.

J'arrive tout couvert encore de rosee

Que le vent du matin vient glacer a mon front.

Souffrez que ma fatigue, a vos pieds reposee,

Reve des chers instants qui la delasseront.

Sur votre jeune sein laissez rouler ma tete

Toute sonore encor de vos derniers baisers;

Laissez-la s'apaiser de la bonne tempete,

Et que je dorme un peur puisque vous reposez.

1.

Here the fruits, the flowers, the folitate fronds,

And here, this is my heart, and you its only beat.

Do not destroy it with your two white hands,

And may your lovely eyes find this present sweet.

I arrive covered all again with dew

Which winds of morning turn icy on my face.

Allow my weariness, that rests by you,

To dream of precious moments that will restore its peace.

On your young breast let me rest my head

Still with your last kisses sounding everywhere;

As quiet comes, after the tempest's fled,

Let me sleep a bit while you are lying there.

2.

Here are the flowers to grace the room we share,

And here the heart empowered only by your sighs.

Please accept them both, and treat with care,

That they may both create that sparkle in your eyes.

I come to you, nervous, battle-scarred,

Where winds of time have left too little space for ease.

Within your arms allow my anxious heart

To dream of precious moments that restore its peace.

On your young breast, let me rest my head

Still with your last sighs resounding everywhere;

As quiet comes, after the sweet storm's fled,

Let me stay within your heart as you are lying there.

WHY THE SEA IS SALT

*

Your laughter is for me

As entangling as the hawthorn tree.

As lingering as the stars beyond

The last stars of dawn.

Your touch is as delicate as the sense

Of lilacs on the winds.

As inerasable as the aftertaste

Of salt, spring rain, and praise.

Your eyes are more silver

Than the moon's reflected velvet.

More golden than the sun

Suspended on the far horizon.

Your love is as strong

As a cherished childhood song.

As persistent and forever

As the ocean's slow, constant measure.

*

The place is well in hand, and all that really

Matters lies within it: all the flats

Are planted now, the marigolds and lilies

Bloom along the edges of the grass,

Tomato plants are bearing fruit, and staked,

The sugar-snaps are tendrilled on the fence,

The weeds are in their usual August place

Beyond the mower's competence, or man's,

And all essential chores are done: the ditches

By the driveway dug, the roofing patched,

The walkway re-cemented, all the bricks

Repointed, and some of the wood is cut and stacked.

The car is tuned and runs as well as ever,

The well is full, and covered against the storm,

The pond is clean, the porch is swept, and over

Everything there lies the proper calm.

Who, when all is quiet in a summer,

Would want another soul to share his slumber?

WHY THE SEA IS SALT

*

"It would be awkward and wrong, and wouldn't match

My fantasies, and I'd be hurt instead;

Or it would be as perfect as my image

And I would fall in love with you," she said,

Knowing more than I did, though still a child,

Nearly. "I think it would be better if we

Just let it stay this way, unfulfilled

Forever—so I will know you wanted me,

And that's a gift I can lock away, in here,

And you will know there was a woman once

Who wanted you so much she didn't dare.

In dreams begin desires, in nightmares, wants."

Farewell, then, my complicated dearest:

Your life is safest, mine bereft and barest.

*

Yes, she loved me: that will be

The legacy I'll always treasure,

Recall on days of drudgery

And fondle, like a charm, in leisure.

There may not be so much of me

The gods of history can measure,

And what there is, as they will see,

Is mixed with pain as much as pleasure.

But let them note, when they confer:

Ah, how she loved me. And I loved her.

SESTINA COLUMBIDAE

How their noise benumbs the summer morning,

The ululations tremulous and unending

Of the mourning doves, somewhere down the Sound

Toward the water, repeating without sense

That same, dull, drawn-out melancholy note

Until it has no pain or sorrow left.

So now I can think calmly of the day I left

You, finally, the way the bright, flat morning

Lay there, unfeeling, as I put the note

Explaining why beside the lamp. The ending

Was inevitable and ugly, but it made no sense

To stretch it out. I went without a sound.

I know poets claim they can match the sound

Of words to meaning: "flat" sounds flat, "left"

Is saddening, "ugly" **is** ugly—as if the sense

Of words created them. But that awful morning

I had no plosive, fricative, gutteral-ending

Words for the bitter anguish in my note.

So it was only a simple, limp note,

About my going back to my wife. The sound

Of "wife," I'll bet, has an edge of cruel, unending

Certainty to it, but by now there's nothing left

In the sound of "hurts" or "sorry" or "goodbye"; the mourning

In my veins could not be conveyed by sense.

And now I know no words could make sense

Of my senseless leaving you, and in that note,

No matter how Shakespearian I was that morning,

WHY THE SEA IS SALT

I couldn't have dredged up the proper desperate sounds—

"Lambent," "willow," "solemn," "cold"—as I left

To tell you so you'd know why it was ending.

Below the doves now comes the true unending,

Slow, growling rumble of the waves. I sense

The doves begin to weary, they turn left

And right along the wire to see whose note

Will be the last, and gradually allow their sound

To wither in the growing heat of the morning.

They, too, are ending with a pain, limp note,

And that dull, soft sound of senseless sense

Is what I'm left with for the long morning.

*

I left her then, at last, and, leaving, spurned

The dreams we'd crafted with our careful art.

I kissed her tears, and said goodbye, and turned

To go throughout my life with half a heart.

WHY THE SEA IS SALT

*

If, then you do not tell your child

About the time when what we'd known

Made your eyes full, your heart wild,

Your blood loud, it will be because

You'll have forgotten, because that was

Your need. But if, when I hold my own,

And tell her everything, it will

Be simply that I remember still.

II

LOSS

*

After all this time not to lose your face,

Almost the press of your lips, not to wake and find

You gone, as you are gone, or be able to replace

What was with forced obsessions of some other kind—

It is so serpentine, entangling, tortuous,

One wonders how the poets could have written of

A complicated, lingering, gnarled thing like this

With such a simple monosyllable as "love."

WHY THE SEA IS SALT

*

I forgo the future, knowing now we'll never

Have what once we thought was ours to choose,

And tell myself there are no dreams to dream.

But the past is too beautiful to lose.

I never believed in ghosts until you left me,

Never knew the world that never was.

You who waked me cannot give me sleep;

You who taught me love now teach me loss.

In darkness now I kiss those broken eyes,

Relive the love we loved, the poems I wrote,

And keep against the dying of the night

The quiet pulsing place along your throat.

SEASONS OF LOSS

1.

Do you ever, in the twilight sighs

Of spring, hear a whisper from a distant hill

As if it were your name, and recognize

It as a cry from one who loves you still?

And would you ever, as you feel that cry

Across your mind, as soft as the winds blow,

Send back to me one time one sign, one sigh:

"I hear, you foolish man; I know, I know"?

2.

This is the summer when no summer comes.

The months are here to bring the sunshine which

They've brought as due these countless millenniums,

But with them no summer comes.

Every weekend there are cold rains.

The weeks are somber, grim with the dim edge

Of winter, against the gray the sun strains,

And on the weekend come the rains.

The clouded skies seldom show the stars.

The moon is dumb remembrance, not so much

A light as a faded place with pallid scars,

And seldom can you see the stars.

There are no birds abroad but the raucous jays.

The nights keep still except for the scabrous scratch

Of crickets, and silence smothers the hushed days,

Except for the squawk of the raucous jays.

The season to a bitter heart succumbs:

Sunshine would be wrong for such a watch

As mine, and the dense, metal darkness numbs,

And this is the summer no summer comes.

3.

The flowers in the wall are withered

Now, dropped with the elegance

Of weary ballet dancers, waiting

Winter's sure, slow advance.

The swamp grass now is so dessicate

The driest delicate winds can make

It rustle: in the waning evening

You hear the sere milk-pods shake.

The monumental oaks are grayed

And empty now, with only dry

Dead leaves around the scuffled base

And vacant veins against the sky.

And green, how simply green, your eyes

That desolate day I said good-bye.

4.

I stand alone on the old decaying pier,

The north winds wizening my cheeks, watching

The ice floes scending in the river where

The seagulls scull and cry, a small one catching

An Arctic gust and riding it high toward

The lowering clouds. I follow its arcing flight,

And think of your crescentine neck explored

By my impatient kisses one April night

So long ago. It happens often: moods

Of insentient serenity are shattered

When some penetrating memory intrudes

Itself, unbidden, as if all that mattered

Happened then. The winds are welcome pain.

The snow, suddenly swirling in my eyes,

Miming tears, seems almost as humane

As sleep, doing its best to paralyze

What it cannot cover. The cold, conveyed

By cold into the very heart of me,

Piercing like a thought, does not invade

My body than your loss more utterly.

WHY THE SEA IS SALT

*

Being with you all the time,

Your joy and strength and laughter all about you,

How could you know the way that I'm

In pain without you?

*

Knowing you are happy makes me glad,

Goes the old lie. In truth, the pain

Is vein-deep, to think that you have had

A willfulness more capable than mine.

For so long I had pictured you alone

And memoried, dead-ended by the day

And finding drink at night, using the moon

As surrogate and salve for far-away.

But now I hear you've gone to a new place,

New job, new man. Your future nullifies

The past that I still keep. I feel my face,

Slowly, cruelly, melting from your eyes.

I wish I could be quite so skilled: instead

I live each day the clumsy stubborn weight

Of what we were, once. And lonely, dead-

Ended, drunk, construct the moon each night.

SAN FRANCISCO

1.

What you did to me, old enough

To be inured, but vulnerable because

Of age and want of some successive love

To ease that age, was devastating, was

As least an 8.3 on the Richter scale.

The papers say today the San Andreas Fault

Is building up another earthquake which,

Geologists think, is strong enough to be called

As dangerous as the one of 1906,

A likely 8.3 on the Richter scale.

No surprise to learn from people how

You've gone to live in San Francisco now.

2.

How can you there, in grays

And browns, forever almost spring, and wet

With Western rain, know

The stark, white ways

A man requires ice who can't forget,

A heart, when breaking, snow?

LUNACY

1.

Not again tonight: I know the color

Of the moon grayed against the plated dawn,

The first-chirps of the birds, the way the sour

Taste of Scotch and poems lingers on.

I do not want you: I do not want the cost

Of seeing you against the uncertain skies

And those last stars. Please believe I've lost

The color of your deep, soft, wounded, sea-green eyes.

2.

I curse the coming night

But that I know without it

Time itself were light,

The day unending noon,

And skies forever clouded

Would show no moon.

3.

I am not bothered by the moon.

Let it push

Its brash authoritarian way across the night,

Deposing all the stars which otherwise would wash

The treetops, glaring with its harsh processional light,

I will not let it subject me.

By now I know

It will not rouse nor pain, it will not signify,

Not that slattern mouth in its perpetual **Oh**

Of lust, no matter how perversely it may try

To raise the memories I've made impotent and numb.

Besides, I know in time the clouds, or dawn, will come.

4.

For some, the rememberings-after are dim spots

In the flimsy summer skies which soon

Recede to their appropriate places

Along with the indistinct faces

Of old teachers, early loves, compatriots

Of war. But for me they are the moon,

The cruel, persistent, pristine moon.

I curse the night. Only while the daylight

WHY THE SEA IS SALT

Lasts can I know no flashes will

Intrude: your eyes too green,

The quiet pulse between

Those thighs, your lips opened in the rite

Of lust. I cling to the light until

The blackness comes, feeding its fill.

I welcome winter. At least within its crude

Numbness, it's amputated bare

Landscapes I can find

Some simple, dumb, blind

Comfort, correlative for the solitude

Of pain. Not that it helps me prepare

For the night—or the night's moon there...

Waiting there, there, out there.

5.

Now this is strange: I saw the moon tonight,

Bright as a head-on train, and in its plays

And shadows, numbed by the harsh, obsessive light,

I saw your face, your lovely unforgotten face.

So I went upstairs and in my attic found

Those negatives of you that you gave me once,

And held them up to the light and turned them round

To try to make your image fit the moon's.

Now this is strange: the faces were not the same;

No matter what I did they would not match.

But suddenly I choked, and cried your name,

And through my tears the contours were exact.

WHY THE SEA IS SALT

*

You poor pathetic lovers, blithely hoping

Life was green and time was full, believing

Love would last beyond this brief incussion,

And chances, like your minds, were always open:

Didn't you understand that Venus wasn't

Coming in on that half-shell, but leaving?

*

One is the shore, and embraces the wash of the sea

As it powers and sweeps through the softening span;

The other the ocean, which swells and subsides as a free-

Running tide till it spends in a rush on the sand.

The one is enduring and constant, as woman must be.

The other sporadic and restless, as man.

WHY THE SEA IS SALT

*

The darkness of the afternoon is heavy
Over the trees. As the clouds thicken, denying
What little sun there was, the air becomes
Opaque, refusing easy breath, and every
Leaf is still. The gray weight benumbs
The birds: even the jays have stopped their crying.

This muffled moment before the storm is worst.
I cannot help it: the memory descends
Of those wild moments that we made together
And once again, suspended, I am submersed
In dreams made anguished by this stagnant weather
And the pain of missing you that never ends.

There is reason for this stillness, the leeched
And ominous emptiness, the sky as cold
As loss. It cannot be that nature's come
Upon this accidentally, unknowing, dumb:
It must be that the word has finally reached
The skies I too have tears too much to hold.

*

How, if I cannot forget you even now,

After all this time, can I forgive

Your letting me fall in love with you, how

Could I pretend there is an amnesty,

An absolution, for the awful memory

With which your carelessness has made me live?

"Amnesty," as you will not know, is from

The Greek *a*—"without," plus *mnasthai*—

"Memory": literally, a forgetfulness. Some

Are capable of it, or say so. I am not.

I remember, weak, will-less, caught

Like some dumb thing that cannot get away.

"Absolution," from the Latin *ab*—"from,"

Plus *solvere*—"loosen," akin to the ancient Greek

WHY THE SEA IS SALT

Lyein—"dissolve." But how could I become

Submerged in the kind of waves that wash away

Our past, when all I have is tears, and they,

Though stinging sharp, are slow, and far too weak?

No: I find no forgiveness for what you've done.

You've kept a man with better things to do

Enrapt in shadows from the setting sun,

The hollows of the lawn you once danced across,

The constant, acrid, yellow taste of loss,

And the insistent, unrelinquished thought of you.

*

What was is past, if present still.

What even might have been has been.

The loveliest loves, and longest, never

Come again.

I know you lie with others now,

You know I envy them the chance.

The helpless cripple is the one

Who loves the dance.

The many painful things that are

The residue of love denied

The dreams that now can never be

Are pale beside.

WHY THE SEA IS SALT

*

The woman who told me of the rabbit in the moon,

One night in the desert in Rhodesia,

Under the whitened acacia trees,

Also said I should pull out before I came,

Both peculiar ways of looking at things.

It is not a rabbit, and it is not,

As childhood insists, a man.

Look close: it is the face

Of a woman in the grimace of ecstasy,

The mouth yawned open awaiting some release,

The dark eyes shut and strained,

As if in pain, as if forever

In that moment when

Someone is pulling out before he comes.

*

You who use other lives, and bodies, now,

Who wake up to the future, cannot know

The comfort of a sunless day, the bitter

Unexpected cold of spring, the amber

Empty hopes of drink, the hard sudden

Force that fills the chest when a violin

Is dying calculatedly to silence.

Laughter and loveliness can fill the gay-green

Righteousness of your days, and you still dream.

How would you ever know the way a tattered

Coat flaps listless on an old, bent pole,

Chasing away no crows where no crops grow,

Or why the aged wolf, a hind leg chewed off

To escape a trap, drags itself half-blind

And not knowing of a lair, across the ragged,

Uncompromising rocks on that far hill.

WHY THE SEA IS SALT

*

Once you plant ivy, getting rid of it

is a lifetime job. Well, yes, you can try to dig

it up by the roots, but there's always quite a bit

you miss, and next spring the leaves are just as big

as they were before: it simply doesn't quit,

no matter what you do; the smallest sprig

becomes a full-blown plant, and all your wit

won't make its roots decay nor leaves renege.

It's yours forever, so they say: those roots

will always mock your surface sweatings. Rest,

let it grow, let its inevitable shoots

spread anywhere they want, let them infest

the entire garden if they want. It suits

some gardens. Some gardeners even love it best.

*

"Hearts will never be practical

until they can be made unbreakable."

—*The Wizard of Oz*

Let them try iron, diamond, stone, the very

Hardest plastics, somehow calculate

How money, science, power, and arcane art

Could build their "practical" most-modern heart,

Yet they will find that any heart they make,

If it knows you, but not how to create

A world where you become its necessary

Unencumbered centerpiece, will break.

WHY THE SEA IS SALT

*

Perhaps I can't say now I loved our life together,

Or even, forced to think about it, her.

But still I loved what I became when I was with her,

And what, those times we loved so well, we were.

*

The greatest gift she gave to me

A woman ever could deliver:

The chance at last to love, to be.

If that's a gift. If she's the giver.

WHY THE SEA IS SALT

*

Again tonight, as cruel as hope, your vision

Penetrates behind my eyes once more,

As changeless and as hard as the collision

Of the sea upon the shore.

I've learned it's better not to fight, and, weary,

Put away the book that does not avail;

It is more inevitable and more necessary

Than the stars are frail.

And giving in, I indulge in feeling lonely,

For a while believing that it is enough

To keep alive the fiction that the only

Lovely thing is love.

III

LIFE

*

"I cannot hope to bring back the
exaltation of that moment: the wonder
of it was like the wonder of an orgasm
in the body of one's beloved."
—Lewis Mumford, *Sketches from Life*

The sweet, sure, abundant showers contain

All that nurtures life and its rebirth:

How great the love the earth must have for rain.

How greater still the rain must have for earth.

THE CONQUEST OF PARADISE

He could be forgiven for thinking it was the East,

Or Cipango, or at least the outer islands of either one,

Although he saw no streets of gold or roofs of jade,

And the people there were brown, not yellow are Polo said,

And nowhere were there men with tails, or fantastic beasts—

He had, after all, spent twenty sullen years obsessed

With the quite unfounded notion the way to the Great Khan,

And great wealth, lay in the passage to the West.

He'd read the ancients: Seneca, of course, and his

Predictions of "ultima Thule," and Mandeville's insane

Inventions, D'ailly's **Imago Mundi** and its fantasies

Of riches beyond the mind of Europe beyond the seas—

In that unstable brain, it didn't take much of this

Before he derived the calculations that served to prove

Cathay was just four thousand miles west of Spain,

An estimate just seven thousand miles off.

He cannot, though, be forgiven for finding Guanahani.

Rescued by its unsuspecting cove, he used

His sword to spill the blood of the first men he saw,

Take seven prisoners, and claim possession for the Law

Of Spain and the Book of Rome, as arrogant as any

Act of humans since the Apple. And in that deed

Five centuries of pestilence and greed were loosed:

Jesus cum Maria sit nobis in via, indeed.

The continents he found were so beautiful and lavish

He himself described them as "an Earthly Paradise,"

And the people there "in all the world the kindest and the best."

And bled by Europe, wrung, crushed, torn, and ravished,

Half the species and a hundred million people dead.

So much for the Captain's noble, blessed enterprise.

Would that he had really found Cathay instead.

WHY THE SEA IS SALT

*

When I take walks I like to make them be

Circumambulatory, and as random as dice,

The principle being that there is so much to see

It makes no sense to see the same things twice.

Out-and-back on the same used path is just

A way of making ruts: the worn-down route

Without surprise is as serendipitous

And venturesome as a suburbanite's commute.

Let others, caged, wear down their I's and U's;

I, haphazard, mind my P's and Q's.

*

Once I rushed to be outside

When a storm started and lightning flashed,

And felt my pores revivified

As I was washed.

But now I reckon more the cost

Of sopping clothes and a cold skin:

Now I think of what I've lost

When the chill's in.

Once I joyed in finding a flood

To cascade, reckless, down in spring,

And all the dangers made my blood

Alive with the tingling.

But now it's sufficient to go out

WHY THE SEA IS SALT

In a one-oared dinghy on a pond:

Enough excitement in a boat

Going round and round.

Once I had affairs with all

The women fortune held in store;

I learned to relish passion and call

It something more.

But, taken one thing with another,

I think by now I've had enough

Of all the stirrings and the bother

Known as love.

*

Blessed are the poor for they shall inherit

The earth, the withered, poisoned, desperate earth,

The venomed, leached, impoverished earth, the arid

Malign terrain despoiled of wealth or worth.

The rich, of course, shall inherit the moon, and when

They overrun their colonies there, will find

Still other planets to settle on again

And watch, at night, the homes they've left behind.

And they will overflow with pride of place

Until, despoiling as is their way, they'll even

Have to flee to ever-farther space

Which they will call, as is their way, a heaven.

And yes, the poor shall inherit the earth, if there is

An earth, and theirs shall be the task to caress it

Back to life, if there is a life. And this,

This, though they will not know it, this is blessed.

DALLAS-FORT WORTH

I think hell will be this way: cold

and airless, plastic, full of strangers, phones

in long unanswered rows, orders called

in tinny flat admonitory tones

as if to children, bored officious guards

with eyes as blank as walls, far-off roars

and rumbles, seats as hard and flat as shards,

cries of babies, unmarked forbidding doors,

and everywhere a cloying, clammy sense

of unnamable anxiety, edged

with fear, as if there were some dark immense

conspiracy to which we all were pledged.

They say it's D-F-W. Might as well

Be any airport in the world. Or hell.

GULF WAR

After W.O.

If in your imagination you could fly

Across those lands and see the bodies lying

Twisted by the road and hear the cry

From those whose leaking blood is testifying

To the unquestioned omnipotence of war;

If you could feel the desert mother's lungs

Breathe, No more, No more,

Across their inarticulating tongues,

My friend, you would not tell without some qualms

To children safe behind their distant border

The old lie, "We are forging with our bombs

A new world order."

TAUGHANNOCK

They don't notice it who go to see

The unrelieved straight-falling tourist sight

And take its stark impulsive force to be

The truest sign of water's own delight,

But farther down the stream where no one stops

The self-same water slows into a pond

As still as glass, and then with a slither drops,

Step by step, in measured blocks beyond,

A sudden frothy foam spreading skirts

Of lathered white around resisting rocks,

Except where a small green bush or two inserts

Itself, illogically, into the interlocks

Of ancient plates, and here the complex play

Of light and dark, smooth and craggy, dry

And wet, bronze, silver, ocher, gray,

Umber, pearl, and beige enthralls the eye

For hours, casting kaleidoscopic spells

That teach us water, in the path it takes,

Is happiest this way, down here, and tells

Us so by the soft, chuckling sounds it makes.

WHY THE SEA IS SALT

*

The snake, as motionless as death,

Stalks its breakfast: stopped, fixed,

It seems incapable of breath

Or quickness. Not one quiver, one twitch,

Betrays its watch: Nothing shows

It different from the walk. Unthinking

Head in frozen, sculptured pose,

Silent tongue alert, unblinking

Eyes forever gaped and hooded,

Wait the calm, unpassioned kill.

If I could be alike cold-blooded,

Perhaps I'd be alike as still.

*

Never mind. Pass by. No, really. Pass.

I am not hurt, nor do I need your arm,

Although I thank you. Really. I am—as,

I think, you see—at rest, and the night is warm,

And, taken all in all, this is not such a bad

Position from which to contemplate the stars....

Your is much more awkward, I might add:

Upright. But still. See Orion there? and Mars,

I think, on the horizon, with just a touch of red?

And there, Aldeberon, perhaps, or Altair,

Or Regulus, or Denebola. I don't much care,

Really. I only want to see them all,

Glistening through all that time, and hear the sound

WHY THE SEA IS SALT

Of their names. Betelgeuse, Wasat, Algol,

Menkalian—ah, just roll *that* around

The tip of your tongue a bit—or try Albali,

Mizar, Rasalhague, Procyon,

Antares, Fomalhaut, Zubeneschamali,

Rigel Kentaurus...Ah, well, I could go on

This way all night, I guess, there are at least

A thousand stars and the Greeks and Saracens

Once named—it was a passion with the East—

And all of them are music. No, again,

Sir, I thank you for your offer, but I prefer

This curbside planetarium, to be

A horizontal Halley, as it were....

Why? Why here? Well, sir, I think that we

Can say *I* didn't choose the spot—it was

Selected for me, more or less, by the wish

Of William Teacher and Sons, bless them…and the because…

Well, did you know there is a kind of fish,

Found mostly in the tropics, as I've read,

That has its eyes, and mouth, and nostrils, all

Together in one place in the top of its head.

No, Sir, I do not jest—I wouldn't call

Myself in the mood—or position—for idle jokes,

It's true: There is just such a fish, which bores

Itself into the sand on shallow beaches and pokes

Its head up, waiting, staring, for hours and hours.

It is called the star-gazer. Really. Well, I,

Like it, though not so nearly well-equipped,

Pay thus my nightly homage to the sky….

Pass by. Pass by. Pretend I've merely tripped

And only lie here long enough to catch

My breath....Or join me, if you wish: there looks

To be some extra room....Ah, there, just watch,

Is that—slightly spinning—is that not Gacrux?

Or is it Sadalmelik, Tuchbah, Merak,

Alioth...Alphecca...Coma Berenices...

Zosma...Zavujava...Caph...

*

There is no solution

In revolution,

As history proves: it merely brings

The same types to the top again.

Full-circle has the consequence

Of wheeling back the same old things.

What's wanted, surely, is devolution,

Dissolution,

Each to each, as citizens.

An end to all those sad, those futile, kings.

WHY THE SEA IS SALT

*

Too much attention focused on his fall—

though quite a fall it was!—

a wondrous yellow flume against the blue,

twirling feathers, some still flaming, all

decaying claws

in shriveling reach against the spiraling flue.

Little wonder most of those below

stood up to stare

and ponder why the incarcerating youth

put on this spectacle. Even though

no horses cared,

the chroniclers, Auden, must have seen some truth,

seen beyond the fall the rise, beyond

the how the why,

sensed the futile is not as the forsaken,

And thought they knew a flesh of purpose found

beyond the sky:

where matters is the trying, not the taken.

THE TIMES BOOK REVIEW

They perform their deeds

Of ignorance in public, weekly, and once

They've vomited do not apologize.

They cultivate the weeds

And cut down the flowers, polish up the stones

And toss out the jewels, preserve in amber…flies.

Are they like velocipedes

Of bookmen, an ancient toy that spins and runs

Around in circles, some useless huge device,

Or more like centipedes,

Busy at nothing, slimy, slow-paced runts

That crawl, aimless, bewildered, not having eyes?

Their power far exceeds

Their competence, and like children given guns,

Destroy what they cannot recognize.

Matched to their misdeeds,

They who cannot sing hear only grunts,

Who cannot fathom truth only lies.

This way madness leads,

The half ones deciding for the able ones,

The blind ones reading for all of us with eyes.

I only wish those breeds

Without the lore would ask themselves just once

Why jealousy gives rights to criticize—

And, shunning then their creeds

Of posture and pretense, declare their stunts

Disbanded, their revels over, say, "Here lies

The TBR, its deeds

Forever buried. Walk softly, for these stones

Are sacred: at last at rest we recognize

Our ordure now at least can fertilize."

*

DEATH SPEAKS:

Pardon me, my lord, but I have come

Looking for your servant. I had seen

Him earlier this morning, in Baghdad,

When I was in the casbah among the plum

And date purveyors, but alas I had

No chance to talk to him. He looked quite green

When he first saw me there and ran away

As if he were afraid.

THE MASTER: Why, yes, he raced

Straight here to me and said he cursed the day

That he was born, for he had run into

You in the market and when you saw him you

Had made a threatening gesture toward him. He

Asked me please to let him have a beast

To ride so fast that he could quickly flee

As far away as Sahmara, where he thought

He would be safe.

DEATH SPEAKS: I see. But that was not

A threatening gesture that I made—it was

A gesture of surprise, not one of fright.

I never expected to see him there—because

I have a date with him, in Sahmara…tonight.

WHY THE SEA IS SALT

*

It is the blatant stare

Of the glaring moon I like,

The bare insistency,

The white so consistent white.

It tells me truth; or lies;

But plain, unsutured plain.

Denuded, with a mouth

Almost wanton, or pained.

Blank, unfired, flat,

Contained in its own peace.

Stark, and dumb, with none

Of the sun's subtleties.

That light, that tyrant light,

That owns and ordains the night.

*

Age is only knowing there is less to live

Than one has lived, and in the stiffening limbs there lies

Much more of love than there is energy to give.

Not merely knowing: but accepting. When the sighs

Of spring, the moon, the dangled hands occur, the skirts

Balloon and beckon before your blue remembering eyes,

Agreeing then, the thought of all that was exerts

More weight than all that might become, deciding then

That there is recurring pain, and even pleasure hurts.

The inevitable and futile fate of men, poor men:

Knowing how, but knowing not, to do again.

WHY THE SEA IS SALT

*

Living is not whatever's done to us,

It's what we do, we claim, pretending

How we write the parts determines how

We give the play a different ending.

Brave stuff, and such a strut as necessary,

Maybe, some pomp to fool and soothe:

More lives sustain themselves by self-delusion,

After all, than do by truth.

But in the gray regretting-time of dawn

It would behoove the credulous

To ask if all our power with the rain

Is quite the same as its with us.

*

When I found it on the footpath, just

A while ago, some small white worms feeding

On its mucous eyes, and at the crust

Around the slit from which it had been bleeding,

It swarmed with zealous, loud blue-bottle flies,

And in its mouth were yellow-jackets, greedy,

Crowding for the carrion sweets. The eyes,

Once I'd chased the scavengers, were needy,

Somehow, and accusatory, and still afraid,

But not of me. I got the shovel, and when

I lifted, the body rolled across the blade

As if just then it had come to life again,

And lay against the handle looking straight

At me. I shuddered, nearly dropping it,

WHY THE SEA IS SALT

Then quickly took it to the woods, its weight

Heavy on my arms, to dig a pit

For some fit ceremony of dispatch.

As I was digging I didn't look at those

Undying eyes, but I could feel them watch

Me working on the place where I would dispose

Of it, and imagined they would be surprised

At such a custom, such a formal giving

Back to Nature what she herself devised,

The dead a grateful homage from the living.

I put the little body in the pit

And took one final look. The fear had gone,

The accusation, replaced by a definite

Uncertainty about what was going on.

But how explain? I filled the pit in swift,

Efficient strokes. But how to name the cause?

I could not know, or say, just why this gift

To earth was necessary. But it was, it was.

EPITHALAMION: SONG OF SONGS

For lo, the winter is past, the rain is over and gone,

The flowers appear once again, the time of the singing of birds

Has come to the land, and the voice of the dove is heard in the dawn.

O my love, let me see thy countenance, let me take in thy words,

For fair is thy countenance, sweet is thy voice, together our vines

Will bear tender grapes. My beloved, my friend, on this day of our bliss,

Come let us go up together to the field where the mandrake dines

And pomegranates bud, for there I will give thee my love and my kiss.

Listen—forth from the hills, the valleys, the regions around,

Come resonant wishes from all of the earth and the people thereof:

May happiness, children, achievement, excitement, and music abound,

But especially, forever, through all that may happen, may love—yes, just love.

*

Apes, they've found, can recognize their own reflection,

Just like humans. Their ability to make this link·

Suggests a certain kind of simian introspection

That hints we may not be as special as we think.

Science discovered not so long ago that apes

Acquire language: with computers they mime speech

By pushing buttons representing certain shapes

And proved apes say—though not in Ape—the things we teach.

Other tests have shown they have a social sense,

Not only of the family but of the communality,

And recognize not only death, but with intense

Preoccupation contemplate their own mortality.

It is perhaps unsettling, learning monkeys can

Do all of this, because it forces us to lead to

This conclusion about our specialness as Man:

We are the only animals who blush—or need to.

*

"From close-up scanning by the Voyager I satellite, Io has now emerged as one of the most remarkable and perplexing bodies of the solar system. It also displays features peculiar to its own history: a white doughnut, as large as Rhode Island. What kind of blow-out or external impact produced the whitish doughnut— perfectly circular but with an irregular dark area inside it?"
—New York Times, March 7, 1979

Oh, I pity her, poor Io, maiden

Loved by Zeus and certainly a lot

Of other lesser gods besides, afraid and

Trembling on the day that Hera got

Wind of what the two of them were up to

And stormed on down to wreak her wild revenge

Before old Zeus had time enough to hop to,

Turning the wretched child, slow inch by inch,

Into a polynucleated heifer.

But nothing, as they say, can last forever:

WHY THE SEA IS SALT

Io, turned by Hera, was turned in turn,

After many centuries of bovine use,

By Gallileo into the inmost moon

Of Jupiter—which is to say, of Zeus.

And that explains why astronomers have found

A huge and perfect circle—what they call

A "whitish doughnut"—on its mottled ground,

With, inside of it, a huge, dark hole,

The mark, it's thought, of jovial nights sublime:

Nobody loses, they say, all the time.

*

The sixth day was the hardest one—

And it was a hard week, mind—

For then He made the living creatures,

Each after its kind,

The cattle and the creeping things,

And beasts of earth, and man,

And as an afterthought, woman,

And then said, "Here's my plan:

You should be fruitful, and multiply,

And fill the earth, and subdue it,

And have dominion over all—

Well, don't just stand there, **do** it—

"Dominion over the fish of the sea

And over the fowl of the air

And over every living thing

That moveth everywhere."

And He saw everything He made

And said that it was good:

And held it should continue thus

As He decreed it would.

Or so the story as it's given

To this day in Man.

I'd like to know the version in Shad,

And Crow, and Orangutan.

*

The Hudson's opulence of color has its own sense

Our senses seldom see: what we call river-green

Is more a slate-blue from the turquoise sky reflected,

The dark flat-grayness of the distant waves is seen

As glinting whiteness when its running through your hands,

The verdant mountain's shadow is purple and mist-complected

In the water's glass, and the yellow sun across the dense

Transluscent surface refracts to blinding silver bands

And gold and copper fragments of a ceaseless dance.

In colors, too, she travels her own way, not man's.

LATE-NIGHT THOUGHTS

Foolish we to think we can

Evade that last eternal crevice

With that ancient lie of man:

Ars longa, vita brevis.

They're not so sad,

Just saccharine,

Those poet's words,

"It might have been."

The saddest words,

When understood

With age, are these:

"I wish I could."

The penis has its own inventions

When it comes to making love,

The heart, for all its good intentions,

Knows not of.

When I reflect how many cells

Remain in what my brain's become,

I take my comfort from the thought:

Cogito, ergo some.

WHY THE SEA IS SALT

*

So much simpler to prepare

For dark eternities in hell

And Sisyphean tasks

Than work for what awaits up there:

"Have you lived life ill, or well?"

The devil never asks.

*

In the end, it is acts of

Clumsy uncertainties

That cause the pain, that fracture

Sculptured, structured ease

And let in confusion's slop.

In the end, better a

Sure full stop

Than an unending etcetera.